WALKS AROUND
Bakewell

10 WALKS UNDER 6 MILES

DALESMAN

Dalesman Publishing Company Ltd
Stable Courtyard, Broughton Hall,
Skipton, North Yorkshire BD23 3AE

First Edition 1998

Text © Martin Smith

Illustrations © Christine Isherwood:
p5 primroses and violets; p10 stoat; p13 dropwort, small scabious,
quaking grass, salad burnet and rockrose; p14 spring sandwort; p17
kestrel; p20 meadow cranesbill and bellflower; p23 kingfisher;
p28 common blue butterfly on ragged robin.

Cover: Lathkill Dale by Martin Johnson

A British Library Cataloguing in Publication record
is available for this book

ISBN 1 85568 145 5

All rights reserved. This book must not be circulated in any form of binding or cover
other than that in which it is published and without similar condition of this being
imposed on the subsequent purchaser. No part of this publication may be reproduced,
stored on a retrieval system or transmitted in any form, or by any means, electronic,
mechanical, photocopying, recording or otherwise, without either prior permission in
writing from the publisher or a licence permitting restricted copying. In the United
Kingdom such licences are issued by the Copyright Licensing Agency, 90 Tottenham
Court Road, London, W1P 9HE. The right of Martin Smith to be identified as author of
this work has been asserted in accordance with Copyright Designs and Patents Acts 1988.

Printed by Amadeus Press, Huddersfield

Contents

Introduction

The ten walks in this book are all set within close proximity to Bakewell. They are designed for the casual walker, the walker with time to spare and for those with young families where speed and distance are not possible. The walks take in some of the finest countryside round Bakewell, the limestone gorges and dales, the gritstone tors and moors. The descriptions and the accompanying maps are sufficient to enable you to undertake the walks safely. However, it is not good policy to walk without an official map, or without the skill to read it, so you are advised to obtain a copy of the OS Outdoor Leisure map 24: The White Peak, which covers all these walks.

None of the walks involve serious climbing, but Bakewell and its environs are not for those who like flat walks, though there are one or two examples. Good footwear is essential and even on the best of days the weather can let you down. A waterproof is a wise precaution. One or two of the walks visit the limestone or gritstone outcrops where children of all ages can enjoy scrambling about and getting the feel of hard rock.

The Bakewell area has a fine network of footpaths and bridleways, most of which are easy to follow. In the area covered by this book, the authority responsible for their repair and maintenance is Derbyshire County Council, with assistance from the Derbyshire Dales District Council and the Peak National Park. Please report any difficulties to one or other of these bodies. All the walks in this book can be reached by public transport. Some of the walks have to be undertaken using a bus at some point. There is information aplenty from the Derbyshire Busline on 01332 292200, or from the tourist information centre in Bakewell on 01629 813227.

Most of the walks pass places of refreshment and these are indicated in the text. Most of the pubs serve food and allow children inside if food is being purchased. In the larger villages there is usually a shop serving ice cream, soft drinks etc. and even in the depths of the countryside you will come across the ubiquitous ice cream van. Nevertheless, a rucksack with a hidden supply of food and drinks is a wise precaution.

Please remember that the countryside is a working environment, someone else's livelihood. You will not endear yourself to the locals by letting dogs or children run riot, by dropping litter, by leaving gates open or damaging stiles and walls. Take nothing but photographs, leave nothing but footprints.

Enjoy your walking.

Chatsworth to Bakewell

Length of walk: 4¹/₂ miles.
Start: Baslow Village Hall (Nether End). Frequent buses from
Bakewell. Parking in Bakewell.
Terrain: Mainly easy going through parkland, but one steep descent.

Catch any of the Sheffield or Chesterfield buses from Bakewell to Baslow and alight at Nether End, by the village hall. Go past the little shop and along the lane, over the Bar Brook. Turn right and follow the narrow track, past the thatched cottage towards Chatsworth, soon passing through a monumental kissing gate into Chatsworth Park. An almost level path leads through the park with glimpses of the "Palace of the Peak" through the trees.

Pass White Lodge on the right and skirt the cricket ground. On the hillside to the left is the Hunting Tower, a survival of Elizabethan Chatsworth. Ahead lies Queen Mary's Bower, another Elizabethan survival, where the unfortunate Mary, Queen of Scots was allowed a brief walk in the fresh air.

The path passes close to the bower before reaching a bridge over the Derwent. Cross the bridge, pausing to admire the classic view of Chatsworth House. Follow the road for 50yds, then bear right along a path which soon rounds a low hillock to reveal Edensor. Cross the road and enter the village by the swivelling gate. This is a classic estate village, well kept and with no two houses the same. It replaced an earlier settlement which was demolished as part of the parkland improvements. It is worth looking round the village, which also boasts a tea shop. The church of St Peter's is particularly fine and in the churchyard are the monuments to various members of the Cavendish family.

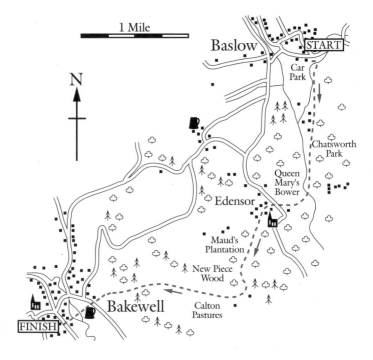

Continue past the north gate of the church to a signpost pointing left to Rowsley. Go left, up a flight of steps. The path bends to the right and forks. Again go left, up another flight of waymarked steps, to a curious stile cum gate on top of the ha-ha wall. A ha-ha is a ditch and wall, designed to keep cattle out, but allow residents an uninterrupted view over the parkland. It is a common device around stately homes, but not so common round a village.

Beyond the ha-ha, bear right, over pathless grass, making for a waymark post. Keeping left of a clump of trees, make for the centre of a much larger stand of trees ahead. Further progress soon reveals that there are two stands of trees and the right of way makes for the gap between them.

The route has been climbing gently and now Chatsworth House comes into view as you look back. Keep just to the right of the large clump of pines, then follow a more distinct path up towards the trees on the horizon. The further you rise the better the view back, with the Hunting Tower perched on the hilltop above Chatsworth.

Still climbing, keep to the right of the fence fringing a newish plantation, then proceed straight ahead, over a couple of terraces, to a stile and gate into New Piece Wood. Here there is an information board and a good opportunity to stop and admire the view, which takes in a considerable length of the Derwent valley, right up to Longshaw. The eastern edges are very prominent and to the left lies Hucklow Edge, topped by the television mast on Sir William Hill.

Go through the wood on the walled track, soon reaching Calton Pastures. To the left is the Russian Cottage, one of the more unusual estate cottages. Follow the track down to a signed "cross-roads". Turn right here and commence a long trot over the Pastures, following an obvious terraced path. Continue straight ahead at the next gate and stile, with the path gradually converging on the fence to the left. After heavy rain this can be a wet and muddy stretch.

The path coincides with the fence at a gate and stile, by a partly overgrown pond. Go over the stile, turn right, passing the pond and soon reaching another stile, signed to Bakewell. Bear left across the parkland. Suddenly Bakewell comes into view below and the view westwards is very extensive. On a clear day the gritstone hills west of Buxton can just be seen overtopping the limestone plateau.

Head towards the double pylon to a step stile, leading into the wood. Here you leave Devonshire territory and enter Haddon Estates, property of the Dukes of Rutland. A steep, rough path descends beside the stream to a cross track. Turn right, cross the stream and then immediately go left, descending steeply again through the wood. This path can be very rough and wet underfoot. Soon it levels out and emerges onto Bakewell golf course.

Follow the waymarks across a narrow strip of golf course, to a stile. Continue downwards along an obvious track, soon reaching a bridge over the Monsal Trail. Cross the bridge and continue down beside the hedge, soon emerging onto Coombs Road. Turn right for about 100yds then go left on the signposted path that leads round the new Agricultural Centre. Cross the mill race, the car park and the River Wye (there are bridges) to reach the town centre and the end of the walk.

Circuit of Stanton Moor

Length of walk: 5 miles.
Start/finish: Rowsley, Peacock Hotel. Frequent daily buses from Bakewell. Parking at old station, just off A6.
Terrain: Field paths and moorland. A taste of wilderness and some rocks to scramble on.

Go down the road opposite the Peacock Hotel, passing the school. Cross the Wye and go straight on at the road junction. After about 500yds, keep right at the fork, climbing gently towards Stanton Woodhouse. Near Stanton Woodhouse, follow a sign on the right, pointing to Stanton Lees. Go through a kissing gate and alongside the wall, soon reaching another signpost, pointing through a gate on the left, to rejoin the lane. Go right, soon reaching the main part of Stanton Woodhouse. Pass through the farm and back into open fields.

Follow the steadily rising track across the field, rounding a shoulder of higher land to a gate. Then follow a signposted path to the left, up the field, towards the trees, soon reaching two gates. Pass through the smaller, right-hand gate, then continue up the field, skirting the lip of a disused quarry, crossing a small field and so reaching a road. Go right here, with the tree covered, rocky slopes of Stanton Moor to the left, the result of long ceased gritstone quarry workings. After about 100yds, turn left up a quarry track. Bear left past the ruined quarry buildings, on a path which soon climbs away through the trees. At the boundary of the National Trust Stanton Moor Estate go right, along a clear path which soon crosses a stream. Continue through woodland, which forks near the lip of another old quarry. Keep left along the more obvious, kerbed path, which heads between two sets of old workings.

The path soon leaves the workings and bears left through much older trees, soon being joined by another path from the right. The route now comes quite close to the edge of the moor, which here falls away in man made crags. There is a good view over the tops of the trees to the eastern moors. Look out for a rock with a large G carved into it; and the date 31/12/15. The moor was stripped of trees during the First World War. Perhaps this is the mark of one of those involved.

Continue along the path, ignoring a stile on the right, and, still following the wall, reach Grey's Tower. The tower was erected by the local landowner, to remind the Duke of Devonshire, a Tory, of the Liberal victory and the 1832 Reform Act. Grey was the Liberal Prime Minister who brought in the Reform Bill. Go round the back of the tower on to the moor. Bear left following the obvious path through the heather, passing various heathr and rhododendron-covered mounds, which are either ancient hut circles or burial mounds.

After about 500yds, keep right at the fork. Soon another path joins from the left. Climb gently, with good views left, over to Winster. On the right is one of the more prominent hut circles. Go straight on at a major crossing of tracks, over the brow of the moor to reach the Cork Stone, shaped like the cork in a champagne bottle, overhung on all sides. On this eastern side, steel hoops have been inserted at intervals to aid the ascent and, more particularly, the descent! Worth a climb, but take great care.

Turn right by the Cork Stone, skirting a shallow quarry, bearing left where the track forks. Soon, on the right and scarcely higher than the path, is the trig point marking the summit of the moor. This is not worth visiting as the view is no better. Cut across the moor through a little patch of birch, keeping to the right at the fork and soon reaching a cross 'roads'. Turn right here through the birch to the Nine Ladies stone circle. Innocuous as these seem in the sunlight, in twilight, with wreaths of mist swirling round, they present a different aspect. Weird goings-on are not unknown at the Nine Ladies.

Leave the circle on the broad path leading away northwards. There is a glimpse of the television mast through the trees to the left. Keep on this broad track, passing through two stiles and fields to the road. Go left, following the lane down almost to the 30mph signs. Turn right, along a signposted track, passing the cricket ground, with a magnificent view up the Wye and Lathkill valleys. Beyond the cricket ground the track passes through woodland before emerging on the Stanton-Pilhough road. Go right, passing a well-built viewing platform on the left.

Just beyond this, at a signpost, go left and descend into the adjacent field, bearing right to a gate and stile. Go straight across the next field, heading for the line of trees marking an old boundary. Follow these to the far side of the field, where there is a stile. The path follows the hedge on the right, finally deserting it to bear left to a stile, just to the left of the gate. Here the path drops into the sunken lane. Turn left and go steeply downhill to Congreave. There is no footpath or verge. Go round the bends, and, at the second left-hand bend, go right, at a footpath sign, passing alongside Dove House Farm, to a gate into open fields. Contour right, with a view across towards Haddon and Calton. The path rounds the nose of the hill before descending left to a stile and stream by a little wood.

Go up through the wood to a stile and into fields again. In the field, bear right, rising to meet the mound and ditch which surrounds Pic Tor, the tree clad hill on the right. An isolated post and notice marks the route. Bear left along a terrace, with the mound and ditch soon diverging to the right. The path carries on downwards to a gate and stile by the river. Here the road is rejoined and it is an easy step back to the Wye bridge and Rowsley.

10

Deep Dale and Sheldon

Length of walk: 6 miles.
Start/finish: White Lodge car park, west of Bakewell on A6. Daily buses from Bakewell.
Terrain: Limestone dale walking, sometimes slippery. Two steep descents.

From White Lodge car park and picnic site follow the waymarked path towards Deep Dale. At the fork in the path bear right, which is the less obvious of the two paths. This soon climbs into a wooded side dale, crossing bands of slippery limestone. Continue up the dale, where the path is quite distinct, until the valley widens out, close to Taddington Field Farm.

Turn right, through a stile, which was clearly part of a sheep dip at one time. Then go left, through the farmyard and onto the lane. Follow the narrow lane across the open plateau with widening views. Soon the lane begins to dip towards Taddington village and shortly reaches a T junction. Turn left into another lane which rises steadily, back onto the plateau again. This lane has more open views than the previous one and soon the aptly named cleft of Deep Dale can be seen to the left. The lane dips to reach Over Wheal Farm, and there the tarmac surface ceases. A rough and sometimes boggy track continues between drystone walls, climbing slightly.

About 100yds beyond Over Wheal, go through a gate on the left and head across the field, keeping to the left of the grass covered mound. Now Deep Dale lies ahead and the steep climb on the far side can clearly be seen, with the gaunt remains of Magpie Mine beyond. Pass the ruined pylon and through a couple of stiles onto the steep daleside. There is no obvious path into the dale bottom, so make your way down with care. The dale bottom is soon reached. If you have judged correctly, you will now reach a stile and begin the ascent.

Climb the steep daleside and then go through a series of fields via gates or stiles. As the path nears Sheldon it veers to the left through a stile, then right again to a gate, to reach the road at the edge of the Sheldon village. Turn left and then right near the first house. The signposted path leads unerringly across fields to Magpie Mine, but if time presses or excessive grumbling has set in, then proceed down the village street and cut out the visit to the mine.

At the mine pay a visit to the information office and have a good look round this fascinating site which has remains of lead mining from the earliest times to the 1950s, and has a history to suit, ranging from murder and ghosts to fortunes won and lost. The ruins of the Cornish engine house and chimney are particularly impressive and the reconstructed horse winding engine is worth inspecting by the shaft of Red Soil Mine.

On leaving the mine retrace your steps for a short distance then take the right hand path through a series of small fields, keeping your eyes peeled for the stiles ahead. They merge beautifully into the rest of the limestone walls. Those with a good sense of direction will emerge in Sheldon, close to the pub. The Cock and Pullet is a new pub, opening only in 1995. Walkers are

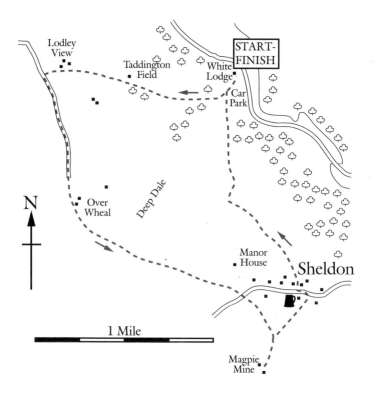

welcomed and both the beer and the food are very good. The earlier pub in Sheldon was the legendary Devonshire Arms, next door to the present inn. The Devonshire sold only mild and that out of pot jugs. Quarts were available for real aficionados. It was also host to the legendary Sheldon Duck, which reputedly flew into a hollow tree and never emerged. When the tree was chopped down the image of a flying duck was found on the bark. This was cut out and preserved for many years.

From the pub walk down towards the church and there turn left along a narrow lane. Follow this lane which soon begins to dip as it approaches an area of overgrown lead spoil heaps. Keep a sharp lookout for a stile on the left and then follow the field path through the workings, soon passing the impressive mine remains on the left. At a T junction of paths/tracks go right. A few fields further on the path reaches the lip of the dale and the edge of Great Shacklow Wood. A steep and slippery descent now follows, until the path bears away to the left. On emerging from the trees the path is waymarked over a band of limestone. Soon the outward route is reached and then followed easily back to White Lodge.

Eastern Edges

Length of walk: 5 miles.
Start: Baslow, Nether End car park. Daily buses from Bakewell.
Terrain: Clear paths with only one significant ascent. Mainly along the gritstone edges with magnificent views. Some grand rock scrambles.

Catch the Sheffield Mainline bus (usually a double decker) from Bakewell (or from Baslow if you've parked there). Alight at Tedgness Road, Grindleford, just beyond the Maynard Arms and the de-restriction signs. Cross the main road and go left, up Tedgness Road. Continue up the road passing some sumptuous houses, then, at the house called High Lodge, go left at the second signpost. The path is signed to Froggatt Edge and Haywood Car Park. The track soon becomes no more than a path with houses to the right and the wood to the left.

At the National Trust sign, the houses are left behind and the path climbs gently through the trees. For about ¼ mile there are no turnings to right or

left to mislead. Then the path forks and a narrower path bears left and continues upwards. Continue on the main, right hand path, which descends slightly before rising again. Another path trails in from the right and you pass an old overgrown quarry on the left. Just beyond, there is a sudden view to the right, down into Grindleford. Continue ahead, soon reaching a gate and Haywood car park.

Skirt to the right of the car park, on a good path, which soon dips sharply to reach a stream. Cross the stream and climb up to the road. Cross the road, with care, and go right, to a kissing gate leading onto Froggatt Edge. The walk along the Edges is one of the best in the Peak District. The first section is through woodland so the view to the right is hidden, though there are occasional clusters of rocks which cry out to be climbed. At a gate, the path

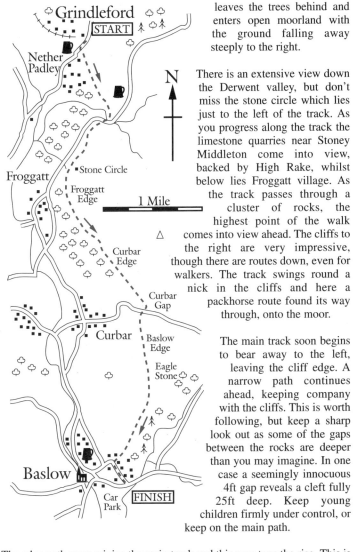

leaves the trees behind and enters open moorland with the ground falling away steeply to the right.

There is an extensive view down the Derwent valley, but don't miss the stone circle which lies just to the left of the track. As you progress along the track the limestone quarries near Stoney Middleton come into view, backed by High Rake, whilst below lies Froggatt village. As the track passes through a cluster of rocks, the highest point of the walk comes into view ahead. The cliffs to the right are very impressive, though there are routes down, even for walkers. The track swings round a nick in the cliffs and here a packhorse route found its way through, onto the moor.

The main track soon begins to bear away to the left, leaving the cliff edge. A narrow path continues ahead, keeping company with the cliffs. This is worth following, but keep a sharp look out as some of the gaps between the rocks are deeper than you may imagine. In one case a seemingly innocuous 4ft gap reveals a cleft fully 25ft deep. Keep young children firmly under control, or keep on the main path.

The edge path soon rejoins the main track and this now tops the rise. This is a fine vantage point, with views back to Longshaw and southwards to

Curbar and Baslow Edges, with the Wellington memorial and the Eagle Stone, whilst further still lies Chatsworth. The broad track leads unerringly to Curbar Gap, keeping some way from the edge, but it is worth deviating to see the views down the cliffs.

At Curbar Gap you reach the road. Just to the left is a car park where there is usually an ice cream van. The track continues on the far side of the Gap, onto Baslow Edge. From here there is a grand view straight up Middleton Dale to Eyam and Tideslow. On Baslow Edge the main track keeps well back from the edge, but a narrow trod bears right, keeping to the lip of the crags. Either route can be followed, but the edge path misses out the Eagle Stone. However there's a chance to remedy that in Walk 10 so keep to the edge for the views.

Having skirted a small disused quarry you rejoin the main path again south of the Eagle Stone. Turn right and follow the rough lane down into Baslow. The track soon becomes a walled lane, which is tarred lower down as it nears the village. When you reach the triangular junction, with the tree in the middle, go left, down Eaton Hill, to reach Nether End. Here you will find various sources of refreshment, the car park and the Bakewell bus stop. If you are feeling particularly energetic you could combine this walk with Number One to make a grand day-long tramp.

Elton and Robin Hood's Stride

Length of walk: 3 miles.
Start/finish: Elton church. Monday to Saturday buses from Bakewell.
Limited roadside parking in the village.
Terrain: Good paths with only one significant ascent, but some good scrambling on gritstone.

Go down Well Street by the side of the church, bearing left at the fork, signed to Youlgreave. At the lane end go through the gate and then left by the wall, bearing right in the next field. This field houses the Elton Ski Tow in winter. At the bottom of the field, pass through the right hand stile, making for Anthony Hill, the rocky knoll seen ahead. Follow the clear path as it dips to cross a small stream, then rises across a series of fields before reaching the Elton to Alport road. In some of the fields the path merely clips the corner, a sure sign of its antiquity, clearly predating the enclosure of the fields. The late Richard Cockerton, in his researches into the Derbyshire Portway, speculated that the oldest route for this ancient trackway would not have followed the course of Dudwood Lane as the medieval route did, but would have kept to the higher and drier land near Anthony Hill. This path cannot be far off that route.

At the road go straight across and through a stile signed to Youlgreave. Pass through an area of scrub and through a stile into fields. The path is not distinct here but it is making a beeline for the brow of the hill where Youlgreave comes into view. Head for a gateway near the right hand end of the field wall and thus locate a stile. Cross the access track that leads to Cliff Farm and go through the gate ahead.

Again there is no obvious path, but you should make for Tomlinson Wood at the far end of the field. As the path

17

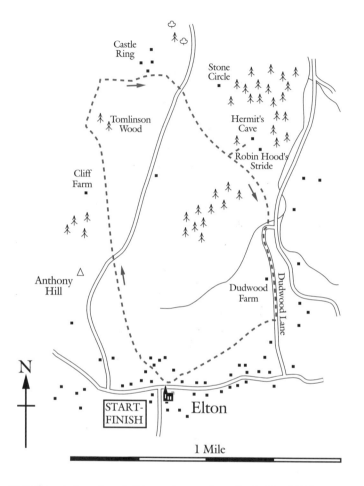

Castle
Ring

Stone
Circle

Tomlinson
Wood

Hermit's
Cave

Robin Hood's
Stride

Cliff
Farm

Anthony
Hill

Dudwood
Farm

Dudwood Lane

N

START-
FINISH

Elton

1 Mile

nears the wood you bear left to a gateway where Castle Ring hill fort comes into view, to the left of Harthill Moor Farm. The fort is an Iron Age structure, built to guard the Portway route.

Follow the path down to a junction of tracks at the base of the hill on which the fort sits and there turn right up a rough and frequently muddy track to the farm. There is no public access to the hill fort. At the main farm access, go right to reach the Elton to Alport road again. Cross the road and go through the stile, making your way across a couple of fields to a gateway to the left of the rocky towers of Robin Hood's Stride.

The Stride is the highlight of the walk and there will be few who can resist the urge to scramble up the rocks. An attempt on either of the two pinnacles is not advised however. The towers have names, that on the left being The Weasel and the one on the right being The Inaccessible. The view from the rocks between the towers is superb, stretching north to Kinder Scout on a clear day.

On leaving the Stride, go through the gate towards Cratcliffe Tor which lies across a flat field. In this field are the remains of a pallisaded encampment, seen well from the Stride. To the left can be seen the few remaining standing stones of Harthill Moor stone circle. At the far end of the field, pass through a stile and then go right, scrambling amongst the rocks and trees to locate the hermit's cave. The carved crucifix and the hermit's sleeping platform can be seen, as well as the ingenious grooves in the rock wall, by which water was fed to the cave.

Leave the cave by the steeply descending path which soon reaches the edge of the wood at a stile. A path follows the edge of the wood back towards the Stride, but then goes left, over a stile into the field. Follow the track down the field to reach Dudwood Lane.

Go straight ahead on reaching the road and climb the narrow lane, soon passing the little hamlet of Dudwood. Just beyond Dudwood Farm, where the climb steepens, there is a stile on the right. Leave the lane at this point and head left across the field, towards old spoil heaps. An indistinct path skirts round the head of some rocky outcrops to reach the back of the Elton playing field, where a track on the left leads directly to the main street. Turn right to reach the church.

Litton and Tansley Dale

Length of walk: 3 miles.
Start/finish: Litton School. Limited roadside parking in the village.
Daily buses from Bakewell.
Terrain: Limestone plateau and dale walking. Good paths but some steep ground.

From the bus shelter by the school, go left along the main road, soon turning right into a lane, signposted to Cressbrook. At the first right hand corner, go left, onto a track, then immediately right, through a signposted stile, into fields. Go down the middle of the field to another stile, then bear slightly left across the next field, climbing gently. There is a good view to the left into Tansley Dale. Continue upwards, still on the same general alignment, soon crossing a track and going over a stile into another field. Still climbing, bear left, making for a stile to the left of the gateway. Go through a narrow field, with a good view over to Wardlow Hay Cop and Peter's Stone on the left. Still keeping more or less to the same alignment you pass diagonally across three more fields, passing through an area of old workings and topping the rise. Thus you will shortly reach the wood which clings to the side of Cressbrook Dale.

Scale the wooden stile into the wood and turn right. The path can be very slippery and the drop to the left is steep though masked with trees. After about 400yds, just after a good view across to Ravencliffe and Wardlow Hay Cop, the path dips and forks. Turn left here, down a flight of steps descending very steeply indeed through the trees. Care is needed in wet weather as the steps are slippery.

At the bottom of the steps the path bears right and soon joins a more or less level track, running along the side of

20

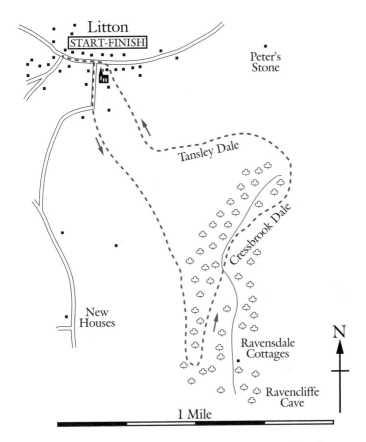

Litton
START-FINISH

Peter's
Stone

Tansley Dale

Cressbrook Dale

New
Houses

N

Ravensdale
Cottages

Ravencliffe
Cave

1 Mile

the dale. Turn sharp left here, passing through a gateway and out into open grassland. Follow the obvious path which soon runs alongside the wood, reaches a gateway and forks. Bear right, leaving the wood and descending steeply into the dale bottom.

Once in the bottom, cross the bridge and enter Cressbrook Dale National Nature Reserve. Please treat this special area with great care. In spring and summer the grassland is a carpet of flowers, including numerous orchids. Do not pick them and do not stray from the paths. The warning sign about mine shafts means what it says. The grassland has been invaded by thorn scrub, which is now being cleared.

Soon the path forks. The lower path continues alongside the seasonal stream, twisting and turning through the trees and scrub, before emerging into the open again, by the remains of Neptune Mine. The path passes across the overgrown spoil heaps and close to the open shaft. Ahead the flat bottom of the dale can usually be crossed dryshod, but in winter a sizable pond forms here and the path deviates to the right, up the bankside, passing another fenced shaft. After heavy rain a stream issues from the drainage level just below the shaft top.

Here the dale is open, with classic limestone scenery. Follow the path to the stepping stones and there go left, crossing the stream, if there is one, and going over the stile, into Tansley Dale. The mouth of Tansley Dale is narrow and shows evidence of previous lead working. Like Cressbrook Dale, this dale, too, is a nature reserve and again the main interest is in the flowers. Pick your times, but not the flowers.

Continue up the dale passing more old workings, until a derelict cross wall is reached. Here the path bears right, following the wall up and out of the dale, soon reaching a stile. Here you leave the nature reserve. Bear right in the next field making for the wall corner and the signpost. Go along the narrow field to a stile by the gate at the end. Climb the stile into a narrow walled track and turn left. Almost at once there is a stile on the right and an obvious path heads diagonally left across the field towards the farm buildings and a final stile. This leads onto Litton main street. Turn left to reach the bus shelter, the school, the Red Lion and the shop selling ice creams.

Monsal Dale and Brushfield

Length of walk: 5¹/₂ miles.
Start/Finish: Monsal Head Hotel. Daily buses from Bakewell. Pay and display parking by hotel.
Terrain: Limestone dale and plateau on good tracks. Some steep ascents.

From the Monsal Head Hotel, follow the waymarks to Monsal Viaduct, taking care not to miss the sharp left turn part way down the hill. The path soon emerges onto the former railway line, now the Monsal Trail. Cross the viaduct and at the far side turn left, leaving the Trail and following a rough track uphill towards Brushfield. The track is an ancient route and is a joy to walk. It ascends steadily, winding its way through the scrub and pasture land. Ignore the route going off to the right and continue ahead, with increasingly wide views all round and into Monsal Dale.

The track levels out and runs along the lip of the dale, with Fin Cop hill fort very prominent on the far side. Brushfield Hough Farm can be seen to the left and soon a track goes off towards it. Ignore this and continue ahead, through a series of gates, eventually coming adjacent to the tree covered slopes above Taddington Dale. The noise of the A6 can be heard below but the traffic cannot be seen through the trees.

An easy stroll leads to the hamlet of Brushfield, where a lane leads down to the left towards the A6. Follow the lane down until it does a sharp left hand bend. Here go right, through a gate and stile into High Dale. Soon the noise of the road is lost in this little-walked dale. Follow the path beside the wall, passing an area of fairly recent workings on the right. In the late 19th century some railway entrepreneurs sought to build a railway from Sutton on Sea to Warrington. In its passage across the country it would have run up High Dale, just over the wall on the right.

Continue up the dale, passing through a bridle gate, still following the wall. A short distance further on, where the wall kinks right, bear right up a side dale, just by a dry dew pond. The path climbs quite sharply, passing through a gap in a cross wall. A little further on the path forks and here you bear left, still climbing gently, to pass through another gap in a wall. Continue through this next field, with a wall on your right and so reach a stile. Turn left along a rough lane for about 100yds then go right at a signposted stile. Follow the wall on the right to the end of the field, where there is a gate. The stile is just to the left.

You now enter an area of old lead workings, with tracks on either side. Cross the workings and go right, following the boundary wall. The path soon swings left and begins to descend, revealing a superb view over Miller's Dale, with Litton Mill in the bottom and the towering cliffs of Water cum Jolly Dale to the right. The path bears right, on a steep slope and so reaches a stile, leading into the nature reserve. Please respect this special area. Don't pick the flowers, they look far better growing here in profusion.

The path descends steeply through more old workings and recently cleared grassland. Pass through a gate and bear right, still descending and soon crossing the Monsal Trail, which was once the Manchester to London main railway line. Turn right once over the bridge and continue the descent along the now obvious path, which zigzags down to a bridge over the Wye. Cross the bridge and thus reach Litton Mill, where there is a cafe. Turn right and pass through the mill complex, following the Monsal Trail signs.

Once clear of the mill, the track passes along Water cum Jolly Dale, with huge limestone cliffs either side. Here the river is more like a continuous pool for it is dammed at Cressbrook. After this delightful stroll the second mill comes into view. This is Cressbrook. The two mills at Litton and Cressbrook have had chequered histories, being famous in their early years for their use, or abuse, of child labour.

Before the mill is reached, turn right, following the Monsal Trail signs and crossing the river again. The path strikes steeply upwards to gain the grassland above the incipient crags. Then an obvious path bears left across the steep slope to reach the former railway line, close to the mouth of Cressbrook tunnel. Turn left here and enjoy a gentle stroll along the Trail, soon passing Monsal Dale station.

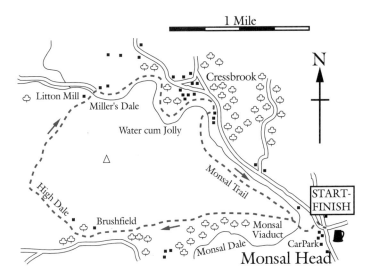

Continue along the Trail, passing through a deep rock cutting, then emerging onto the short embankment before the grand Monsal Viaduct, which you crossed earlier. At this point, the proposed railway from Sutton on Sea would have been above you, for the promoters envisaged a 300ft high viaduct at this point. Not for nothing was the scheme described as "the final flowering from the lunatic fringe of railway mania". Cross the viaduct and go left, up the path back to Monsal Head, where there is a cafe, a pub and usually an ice cream van. Well earned refreshments.

Over Haddon and Lathkill Dale

Length of walk: 5¹/₂ miles (6¹/₂ miles if the extension to Conksbury Bridge is included).
Start/finish: Over Haddon car park. Sparse Monday to Saturday bus service from Bakewell.
Terrain: Dale walking at its best, but some steep descents and ascents.

From the car park turn right on reaching the road and follow the lane steeply downhill, passing the ice cream shop and the church. At the bottom, by Lathkill Lodge go straight on, crossing the river, if it is there, and ascending the steep track on the far side. This zigzags through woodland, then enters fields. Head left across the field towards Meadow Place Grange, the "grange" place name deriving from an old monastic settlement. Pass through the gateway between the two ranges of buildings, through another gateway before emerging into an open area flanked on three sides by buildings. Meadow Place Grange, an impressive building, is just to the left.

Ignoring the gate and lane leading away to the left, go straight on, over a step stile and into a walled, muddy lane. This soon passes through another gateway into open fields. Keep by the right hand wall, passing a signpost and following the route to Middleton and Moor Lane. Continue by the wall to another signpost, then bear left across the field, with the occasional marker post as a guide. At the next stile, bear left across a large field, making for a stile in the top corner, not the more obvious gate. Continue to bear left in the next field and so reach a signposted stile that leads out onto the road. Turn right.

Stroll up the road, which used to be the Bakewell to Stoke turnpike. Take care, for although there is usually a verge, the road is narrow and is used as a short cut by locals. Running almost parallel on the left is the line of trees that marks the site of Long Rake Mine. As you reach the top of the hill, the line of posts in the field on the left indicate the start of the old open cast workings.

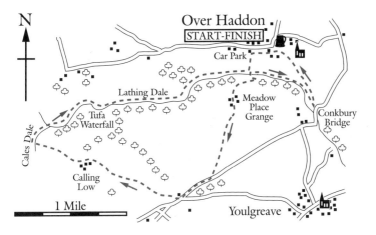

At the road junction, go over the waymarked stile on the right and bear left across the field. Head towards the pylons, bearing right at the next stile and left at the next one. A couple more stiles lead into Low Moor Plantation. Pass through the trees to a stile, skirting to the right of Calling Low Farm. Go through a couple of kissing gates into another plantation, soon emerging into fields again.

Now the cliffs of Lathkill Dale can be seen to the right and ahead lies the deep cleft of Cales Dale, with Monyash and One Ash Grange on the far side. Descend through fields to the edge of Cales Dale which is a National Nature Reserve. A steep and slippery descent now follows. Take care. At the bottom of the slope, turn right and go down Cales Dale to its confluence with Lathkill Dale.

Cross the bridge which sometimes spans a river, but often doesn't, and turn right, below the impressive cliffs. Follow the riverside path, soon reaching a waterfall where the Lathkill plunges over a ledge of tufa rock. This also marks one of the main resurgences of the River Lathkill, which emerges from a low cave at the base of the fall. In dry weather the waterfall is absent as the river goes underground and in very dry conditions it has been possible to penetrate the cave. Even if the opportunity presents itself do not venture in as such expeditions are only for experts. Continue down the dale, soon reaching the remains of an old mill and entering dense woodland. On either side are the remains of old lead mines and wheel pits, for this area was heavily worked during the 18th and 19th centuries.

Soon the path emerges into a more open area, across which marches a line of stone piers, the remains of an aqueduct that served Mandale Mine. The mine can soon be seen to the left and is worth a visit, but not too close an inspection. By the side of the main path, close to the mine, a stone lined tunnel emerges. This is Mandale Sough, a drainage level built to unwater the mine. There is usually a steady flow of water from the sough, but sometimes it is dry. Again, the advice is not to explore too closely.

Continue down the dale, noting a couple of short trial levels in the bankside on the left. These are likely to prove irresistible for children and inquisitive parents. At Lathkill Lodge the outward route is rejoined. Turn left here and climb the lane back to Over Haddon.

If you are still feeling energetic, and have another mile left in you, don't turn left at Lathkill Lodge but turn right and then left, following the path past the house with, possibly, a river to your right. Looking left into the garden you will see a pump. This stands on a shaft into Lathkill Sough, another drainage level. Soon the main Lathkill resurgence is reached, where the river emerges and forms a broad, deep stream. Well worth a visit.

Follow the riverside path to Conksbury Bridge and there turn left, up the road, for a short distance, before turning left again, through a stile, signed to Over Haddon. An obvious path climbs steadily through a series of fields to emerge right by the pub. The village car park lies at the far end of the main street.

Rowsley to Bakewell

Length of walk: 3¹/₂ miles.
Start: Peacock Hotel, Rowsley. Frequent daily buses from Bakewell.
Parking in Bakewell.
Terrain: Easy walking on green lanes and minor road. One significant ascent.

Catch the bus from Bakewell to Rowsley and alight at the Peacock. From the bus stop, go right, up Church Lane, passing the village well on the left. Rowsley once belonged to the Duke of Rutland and the estate still has a considerable influence over the village. Continue up past the church of St Katherine's to the last houses in Rowsley. Nearby is a seat which offers a respite from the climb, though you shouldn't really need it at this stage. The view down the valley is a good one, though.

Soon the lane deteriorates into a rough track, though this was once the main road to Bakewell. At the trees the lane turns sharp right and climbs more steeply, soon reaching a fork. Follow the left hand path, passing a metal barrier. The way is now almost level, though frequently muddy, through Bouns Corner Wood. Soon there is a short rise and the track emerges from the wood, into the open. Here there is a good view to the left, across to Pic Tor and Stanton Moor. At the T junction of tracks, go straight on. The track now begins to descend, soon reaching another metal barrier and a three way junction. Bakewell can be seen ahead.

Take the middle of the three tracks which now begins to descend. This is a quiet, little visited valley, with the wood rising steeply away to the right and the narrow walled and hedged lane dropping gently towards Coombs Farm, which is reached in about ¹/₂ mile. Here the track becomes a tarred lane, which, still descending, soon reaches Coombs Viaduct.

The viaduct used to carry the main Manchester to Derby railway line until its closure in 1967. Pass underneath the viaduct and then turn right, following the signs for the Monsal Trail. The path scrambles up the embankment onto the former railway line. Turn left at the top and follow the Trail for an easy and pleasant mile to the former Bakewell station. The route

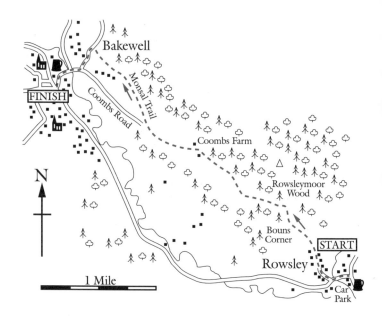

is mainly on embankment so there are good views across the valley and towards Bakewell. The Trail passes under a bridge carrying the Chatsworth to Bakewell path over the line. On the right is the golf course and to the left, in the valley bottom, the famous Bakewell Showground, home of one of the biggest agricultural shows in the country.

Soon the station is reached. The platforms are still intact but the space between them has been filled in so the Trail rises and passes under the road bridge. This is half filled with a mound of earth, put there in a vain attempt to stop the bridge moving. This part of the line was built through shale and there were constant problems with embankments, cuttings and structures slipping. Beyond the bridge lies the station building, a fine example of 1860s' station architecture. Leave the Trail just beyond the station building and go left, passing through the car park to reach Station Road.

Descend Station Road, which also shows signs of slipping down the hillside, and soon reach Bakewell Bridge. Cross the River Wye to reach the town centre and a well earned chance of refreshment.

Wellington and Nelson

Length of walk: 4 miles.
Start/finish: Bus stop at Robin Hood pub on A619 Chesterfield Road east of Baslow. Daily buses from Bakewell. Public parking adjacent to pub. Do not use the pub car park or the roadside.
Terrain: Good paths but some quite rough underfoot. One significant ascent and some good scrambling.

From the bus stop, go down the main road for a short distance to a signposted stile on the right. Go over the stile into fields, soon crossing a terrace, which marks the line of the old Chesterfield to Baslow road. The path climbs up through the rough pasture land alongside Heathy Lea Plantation, soon topping the rise where a view opens out to Birchen Edge on the right, with the Nelson monument on top. To the left there is a steep drop to the valley of the Bar Brook and then over to Eaglestone Flat and the Wellington memorial. Note the stand of trees that make up the initials E R. These were planted in Coronation year.

Pass through the narrow gateway and continue along the obvious path, soon beginning to descend through the birch woodland that lies below Gardom's Edge. A pleasant and easy stroll soon leads to a stile that gives out onto the main A621 road close to Cupola Cottage (a cupola was a lead smelt). Cross the road with care because it is both busy and the traffic moves fast. Go through the stile opposite and descend sharply to cross the Bar Brook. The path then rises steeply, beside a bungalow, soon entering rough ground, an area known inappropriately as Jack Flat.

Climb the obvious path which soon encounters even steeper ground and swings left to avoid it. Continue upwards until you encounter a much wider track and here turn right. Ahead can be seen the Wellington cross and the Eagle Stone. The ascent of the stone was once the test of manhood for Baslow youths. It looks deceptively easy, but it isn't. However, there will be few who are able to resist an attempt. Duly elated at your prowess, or suitably dejected by your failure, make your way across the moor to the cross, which was constructed to commemorate Wellington's victory at Waterloo. It is a grand viewpoint and a good place for a rest.

From the cross, continue along the broad track that leads north across the moor. This used to be the main road from Sheffield to Baslow before the present main road was built. It is still officially a public road. The track leads easily to the Curbar Gap road. Here the old road went straight on and its course can be seen as a series of grooves across the moor, leading down to a clapper bridge. However, you turn right, following the road down to Clod Hall cross roads, taking care as there is no footway. Cross the Bar Brook again, noting the pool on the right which was the reservoir for another lead smelting mill. Go straight on at the cross roads and then immediately right, through a stile onto the moor.

Ignore paths bearing off to the right and instead follow the track leading almost due south, making for the northern end of Birchen Edge, which can be seen ahead. When the path reaches the base of the edge it forks. Either route will do, the lower is the easier, but the upper path scrambles to the top of the edge and commands grand views.

Continue along Birchen Edge, which is normally festooned with climbers. Soon the Nelson memorial is reached. This commemorates the admiral's victory at Trafalgar. Three of the more prominent rocks are named after ships of the British fleet and many of the climbs have nautical names, like Powder Monkey Traverse.

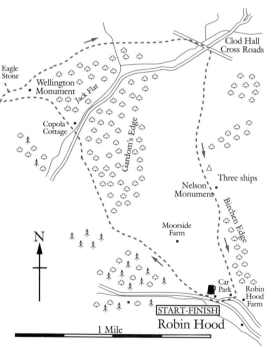

The path continues along the edge to a dip, where a small gully leads down to the right and rejoins the lower path. Bear left here and soon reach the Robin Hood pub.